FOUR WOMEN

Here are four —
There are many more.

CONTENTS

NANNY OF THE MAROONS

Nanny Town is in the mountains of Portland, Jamaica.
You will also find it on maps as Moore Town.
A hill called Bump Grave marks the spot
where the founder of the town is buried.
She died over 200 years ago
and few know the story
of her wars against the British.
But Nanny's deeds cannot be forgotten,
because she fought to be free.

Nanny's roots were in Africa.
Her family was from the Ashanti people.
Their land is part of modern Ghana, in West Africa.

In Jamaica, she and her brother Cudjoe
led the Maroons.
"Maroons" is the name given to the Africans
who refused to be slaves.
When they were brought to Jamaica,
they escaped to the mountains and forests
where they could live in freedom.
Nanny settled at Old Nanny Town
in the Back Rio Grande Valley.
This was in the 1690's.

At that time the British, French and Spanish
were fighting each other
to control the Caribbean.
The British were tightening
their grip on Jamaica.
From their mountain bases,
Nanny and Cudjoe resisted British rule
for nearly half a century.
Nanny led the Windward Maroons.
Cudjoe led the Leeward Maroons.

Nanny ruled as an African Queen
and carried on the African culture
and traditions among her people.
For example, there was great respect
for women and children.
When there was fighting,
they had their own safe places,
known as Girls' Town and Women's Town,
in the John Crow mountains.

As an African leader,
Nanny was also a High Priestess.
She planned her wars against the British
using her spiritual powers
to find out the best time
and the best place to attack.
She also knew
how to prepare warriors for battle,
with ceremonies and charms
to protect them and weaken the enemy.
Her knowledge made her famous
as an "Obeah Woman."
She gave her orders in battle
using the "abeng", the Maroons' horn.

After many years of guerilla war
Cudjoe was ready
to make terms with the British.
Nanny wanted to go on fighting.
In 1737 she took a vow on Pumpkin Hill
to fight the British to the death.
But she could not carry on alone.
In 1739 she agreed to a Peace Treaty.
She and her warriors came
to meet the British
wearing the teeth of dead British soldiers.
In the Treaty, the two groups of Maroons
won rights to their own lands
where they could live how they wanted.
This was when Nanny founded New Nanny Town,
which is on the map today.

The memory of Nanny
is very much alive in modern Jamaica.
Her spirit lives on,
watching over the lives and liberty
of her people.

Ray Uter

SOJOURNER TRUTH

It is hard to know where to begin
the story of SO-JOUR-NER TRUTH's life.
Let's begin in the middle.

In 1843, a black maid called Isabella
spoke to her God within.
Isabella asked why
she was in this world.
Was it just to wash and clean
and be a servant to her white masters?
Or was there more to life?
A voice answered.
It said that there *was* more to life.
It said also that her real name
was not Isabella.
Her real name was Sojourner Truth
(a sojourner is a traveller).

A few days later, Sojourner Truth
set out on the travels
which helped to shake off
the chains of slavery in America.

She was poor, she was black,
she was a woman, she was alone.
She was not afraid.

Let's talk a bit about her early life.
When she was known as Isabella
both of her parents were slaves.
By the time she was a teenager
she was with her third owner.
She was then married to Thomas,
an older slave, and had five children.

The father of some, if not all, of her children
was her owner, John Dumont.
Dumont's wife made sure
that Isabella was often whipped.

When she was twenty-nine years old,
she ran away.
She took one of her children with her.
Luck was also with her.
A white family took her in
and then paid Dumont for her freedom.

She started working as a maid.
She was free, but not happy.
She was lonely.
She missed her children.
She wanted to go back.
It was then that she heard
the voice for the first time.
It told her that God was everywhere.
"There is no place that God is not."
Her heart was full.

She now moved to New York City
with her son, Peter.
She worked as a maid
and went to Church for the first time.
She wanted to know
what the Bible had to say,
but she could not read.
So she started to pay children
to read to her.
She used children because
adults always wanted to tell her
the meaning of the Bible.
She wanted to find her own meaning.

Isabella was now a member
of a strange religious group,
set up by her employer.
A scandal broke out
and she found herself in trouble.
A rich business man blamed her.
She decided to sue him for slander.
To the surprise of everyone,
the black woman won the case
against the rich white business man.

Isabella now took a hard look at her life.
She was forty-six years old.
Her son Peter had gone to sea.
New York City was a "Babylon," she said.
It was now that she asked
if there was more to life
and set out on her travels.
She left Isabella behind
and became Sojourner Truth.

She walked to the North.
She began to hold meetings,
at which she not only spoke,
but sang as well.
Her understanding of the law and the Bible
amazed the experts.
"You read books," she often said,
"but God himself talks to me."
She always started her speeches with
"Children, I talk to God
and God talks to me."

It takes great courage to speak out.
Back in those days, it took greater courage
for a woman to speak out for women's rights.
And it took the greatest courage
for a black woman to speak out
for women's rights and against slavery.
Sojourner Truth spoke out –
with great passion.

One man said to her,
"Old woman... I don't care
any more for your talk
than I do for the bite of a flea."
She answered, "Perhaps not,
but the good Lord willing,
I'll keep you scratching."

Sojourner had found her calling.
The next forty years of her life
saw her travelling all over America.
She was the first black woman
to speak out in public
against slavery and for women's rights.

At one meeting, a doctor said
that Sojourner was a man.
She answered, “My breasts have suckled
many a white babe,
even when they should
have been suckling my own...
It is not my shame but yours
that I should do this.
Here, then, see for yourselves.”
She tore open the front of her dress
and asked the doctor,
“Do you wish also to suck?”

She travelled here, there and everywhere
to speak her truth.

She even called on President Lincoln.
Even after slavery was ended
she still spoke out:
"So much good luck to have
slavery partly destroyed – not entirely.
I want it root and branch destroyed.
Then we will all be free indeed."

She often found herself alone.
At one women's rights meeting
no-one wanted the black woman to speak.
The men there were winning the argument.
Then Sojourner stood up.
Some of the other women shouted
"Don't let her speak! Don't let her speak!"
Sojourner kept her cool.
She waited for quiet
and then started to speak.
"Children," she said,
"that man over there says
that women need to be helped into carriages
and lifted over ditches...
Nobody ever helped me into carriages
or over mud puddles...
And ain't I a woman?
Look at me! Look at my arm!

I have planted and gathered into barns
and no man could head me –
and ain't I a woman?
I have born'd five children
and seen most all sold off into slavery
and when I cried with mother's grief,
none but Jesus hear –
and ain't I a woman?"
She now pointed to a priest.
"Then that little man in black there,
he said women can't have
as much rights as man,
'cause Christ wasn't a woman.
Where did your Christ come from?
From God and a woman!
Man had nothing to do with him!"

She was nearly ninety years old
when she died. She always said
that death was like walking
from one room to another.
At three in the morning of November 26, 1883,
she set out on her last travels.
“I ain’t gonna die, honey.
I’se going home, like a shooting star.”

Frank Forde

MARY MCLEOD BETHUNE

A WONDERFUL STORY ABOUT A GREAT BLACK WOMAN

Her name was Mary McLeod Bethune.
She was born in 1875 in the American South
and died in 1955.

She was the last of seventeen children.
Her mother shouted for joy
to know she was born a free child,
because it was at the time
of the end of slavery.

From the age of nine
she was picking cotton,
for there were no schools
for black children.

One morning a lady came to her house
and from that day her life changed.
She started to go to school every day.
Each day she walked five miles to school
and five miles back
with her pail of milk and some bread.
She was very happy.
She remembered everything
that was taught her.
When she finished her dinner,
she taught her brothers and sisters
what she had learned.

She went on to study English,
Latin, Science and Mathematics.

In an old box at school
she found a chapter of the Bible.
It read, "Whosoever believeth in me
shall not perish."
She was thinking about it all the time.
Scales dropped from her eyes.
Fear moved away.
Light came flooding in.

The word "Whosoever" stuck in her mind.
To think no rich, no poor,
no whites, no blacks –
everyone has got a chance.

She was now fifteen
and finished her time at school.
Having nothing to do,
she went back in the cotton field.
But she was getting thirsty
for more education.
She started praying
that God would open a way for her
and so He did.

There was a white dressmaker
who paid for the rest of her education
so that she had the confidence
to seek missionary work in Africa.
Although she was turned down
because of her age,
she was able to chair
many different functions and meetings.
She was paid for the work she did.

With the money she earned
she started saving
to pay off her father's mortgage,
which hung on for a number of years.

A few years later she started to teach.
There she met her husband
and had a son.

After staying away for a while
to look after her son,
she began to get restless.
She wanted to help her people.
She went to a beautiful village,
called Daytona Beach, in Florida,
where they were building a new railroad.
She saw a shabby old house
and rented it for eleven dollars a month.
Although she didn't have
but a dollar and a half in the world,
she took the chance
and the owner trusted her
until the end of the month.
She stayed at her friend's house
and started to beg
for the repair of the old house.
She spoke in churches
and asked the ministers
to let her take up collections
to help pay for the repair of the place.

In that old building she opened a school.
It started with five girls and one boy.
The boy was her son.
The parents paid her fifty cents a week.
She burned logs
and used the charred splinters for pencils.
The children used elderberry juice for ink.
Mary, as they called her, begged for brooms.
She begged for lamps.
She begged for books.
She searched the rubbish dump
for old chairs, old boxes to make desks
and things to make shelves.
At the back of a hotel
she found pots, plates and sheets.
She used corn sacks for mattresses,
for the school started taking boarders.

After some time
she began to be very worried.
The school was overcrowded.
She started begging again,
with her mouth, with letters
and with prayers.
She made cakes, buns, candy
and ice-cream to sell.
She bought a piece of land
and decided to build a college.
The land was used for dumping,
so they called it "Hell's Hole."

One of her begging letters
went to a white man
who thought she was a white woman.
She was choked with amazement
when he gave her a big start.

With the help of many, many people
she was able to build
"the college on the dump-heap."

She went further by building
a hospital as well,
for there weren't any
where blacks could go.

She gave praise to the Almighty
for the wonderful things
that he had done.
She named the college
the Bethune-Cookman College
and it is still very active until this day.

In 1934 Mary got a government job.
She was in charge of
an education programme for black youth.
So she did as she had written:
"I am my mother's daughter
and the drums of Africa
still beat in my heart.
They will not let me rest
while there is a single Negro boy or girl
without a chance to prove his worth."

Virginia McLean

faces exile
of a blood transfusion, and young Claudia volunteered.
This created a stir throughout the hospital on the question of "black blood" and "white blood." The Italian girl received the transfusion nevertheless—and became a lifelong friend of Claudia Jones.
On her recovery, Claudia started on the usual round of seeking work —first in a laundry, then in a factory, finally as a salesgirl in a shop. About this time she first heard Communist and Young Communist League street-corner speakers — they were dealing with Mussolini's invasion of Abyssinia in those days.
WEST INDIAN GAZETTE
CARIBBEAN NEWS
AUG.–SEPT. 1964
6d.
CRY PEACE—
THEIR CRY IS HEARD!
CLAUDIA JONES, Editor of the West Indian Gazette

CLAUDIA JONES

A child was born on 21 February 1915.
Her name was Claudia Vera Cumberbatch.
This little girl grew up in a country
ruled by the British colonial government.
The Trinidadian people were poor
and were treated badly
while the white plantation owners lived
a happy and comfortable life.

Claudia's parents worked hard.
They wanted to leave Trinidad
for a better life in America.
So they saved their money
until all the family had their fare.

Claudia was 8 years old
when the family moved to America.
They settled in Harlem.
A lot of African people lived in this area.
These Africans had lived in America
since slavery days.
The Universal Negro Improvement Association
(the UNIA for short)
also had its headquarters in Harlem.
This organisation was led by Marcus Garvey.

Claudia's parents continued to work hard,
but sadly their situation had not changed.
They had to put up with more racism now.
This was called "Jim Crow" racism.
Jim Crow racism meant that
white people lived in the best houses
and had all the office jobs up town,
while black people lived
in the slums down town –
and were forced to work
long hours for very little pay.

Claudia's own family paid the price
for living in such bad conditions
when sadly Claudia's mother died at work
over her sewing machine.
The children would never see
their mother again.
Claudia's father would never see
his wife again.
The family was bitter.
America did this to them...

Soon after the death of her mother
Claudia left school to look for work.
She was determined to do
something about Jim Crow racism.

There was no point in just complaining
to friends and relatives.
It was at this early age
that Claudia decided to find out
why her people were being treated so badly –
and find a way to stop it happening.

By 1934, aged 19,
Claudia had an understanding of politics.
She wanted to find out more.
So she joined the Youth Section
of the Communist Party (CP for short).
At this time Claudia worked for
a black newspaper during the day
and the CP in the evenings.
She was also studying to be an actress
in whatever spare time she had left.

In 1936 Claudia was awarded
a place to study drama.
She turned the place down
to work for the Daily Worker newspaper.

In 1939 the Second World War broke out.
Claudia continued her work
to better the lives
of poor working class people.
She was very committed to her work.
By 1941 she was a full-time politician.
It was during this time
that she wrote about Adolf Hitler,
saying that there should be
no compromise with him,
because he believed in slavery.
Only people with blonde hair and blue eyes
would benefit from his rules and regulations.
Claudia went on to say that everyone
was fighting together in the war.
There was no need for race hatred...
At this time there were such heroes
as Don Miller and Joe Louis,
two courageous black men
who set an example
of what black people could do
if they were given the chance.

After the war, in 1945,
it was a different story.
Black people were treated as before.
All the black heroes were forgotten.
They went back to the ghettoes
and back to the low paid jobs.

Black people made their feelings known
through the Communist Party
and through their own organisations.
They were sorry
that the end of the war did not bring joy.

Instead it brought the sadness and hardship
that black people knew before the war.

The US Government did not like the idea
of the Communist Party helping black people.
The CP was prepared to defend
working class people, black and white...
This did not please the government,
so they made laws against the CP
and laws against immigrants.
This period in history
was called the "McCarthy Era" –
because it was a Senator JR McCarthy
who said that certain members of the CP
were trying to overthrow the government.

During the McCarthy Era
a lot of people were sent to jail.
Some were executed ?
and some were deported
and sent home as illegal immigrants.

Claudia was sent to jail four times.
Because of this she became ill
with a heart condition.
There were pleas to release her
on health grounds,
but the government would not hear of it.
They were determined
that Claudia would finish her prison sentence.
After serving her sentence,
on 22 October 1955,
Claudia was released from jail
and sent to England on the very same day.
Her native Trinidad
would not have her back.
The colonial government there
was afraid of what she might do.

During her time in the UK,
Claudia took part in organising
the first carnivals in London –
after the riots in 1958.
She also started the West Indian Gazette,
a newspaper for black people in Britain.

Claudia had lived in three different countries
and in each country
black people were oppressed.
The UK was no exception.
In 1962 the British Government
introduced the Immigration Laws.
Black people were either denied
the chance to enter the country
or deported as illegal immigrants.
For Claudia this was
a repeat of the McCarthy Era.

Claudia was a well-respected woman
and well-respected politician.
She was invited to conferences
all over the world.

In August and December of 1962
Claudia went to the USSR
as a guest of a Soviet women's magazine.
She also went to Japan in 1964
for a world conference
against nuclear weapons.
Claudia also travelled to China
and spoke at conferences
on different subjects
including peace and world unity.

Claudia spent ten years in the UK
before her heart condition
claimed her life at the age of 49.
She is buried next to Karl Marx
in Highgate Cemetery, North London.

Women all over the world
remember Claudia Jones
as a strong, courageous woman.
There is a
Claudia Jones Black Women's Organisation
which has clubs all over Britain.
Claudia Jones is truly
one of the many great black heroines
of our time.

Lesnah Hall